The Pocket Pep Talk

by Jill Spiegel
with
Joe Brozic

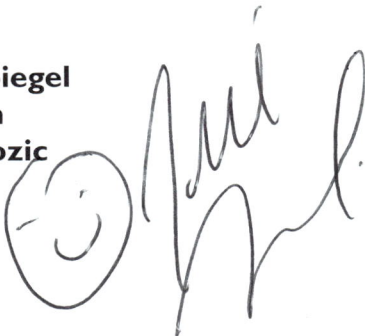

The Pocket Pep Talk
Copyright © 1997 Jill Spiegel
All rights reserved.
Reprint 2002

ISBN 0-9643325-1-5

published by: Joe Brozic
               Goal Getters
write to: Goal Getters
               3943 Chowen Ave.
               Minneapolis, MN 55410
phone: 612-925-5814
fax: 612-922-8241
website: www.Flirtnow.com

Printed in the United States of America
Written and Illustrated—Jill Spiegel
Edited—Steve Lastavich

Jill Spiegel, Motivational Entertainer and
author of "Flirting For Success" owns Goal
Getters with her business partner and
husband Joe Brozic.

The Pocket Pep Talk

Oh hi!

I'm so happy to see you!

You came by at the perfect time.
Let me fill you in. . . .

See, just a little while ago,
I was feeling down.

As you can tell,
I'm not like all the other books.
I don't have many pages
or a lot of words.

Now when I first arrived at the bookstore,
I felt proud.

I thought,
even though I'm not as big
as the other books,
I have my own strengths:
I'm compact and easy to read.

I just know someone will buy me
right away!

I was feeling confident until . . .

"Hey Pocket Pipsqueak, or whatever
your title is, no one will ever buy or
read you. You're so tiny and plain!"

Once the big books spotted me sitting on
the counter, they scoffed at me,

"You'll never make it in this business."

I tried to turn the other cover
and ignore them,

but I have to admit,
it hurt.

Then,

"Hey Pocket! Don't worry.
Don't let those stuffy books get to you."

"Who said that?" I whispered.

"It's me! The little calendar to your left!"

I turned around and sure enough there she was on the counter next to me.

"Listen Pep Talk,
those big books once tried to scare me."

"They've been on that shelf a
long time. . . .

they're sure that they
have the most text,

certainly more than you."

And then she said,

"But I believe in you, and I believe
in me too! Let's stick together!"

"It's a deal!" I smiled.

Calendar's friendship made me feel so
much better.

"Hey Pocket, maybe the same person will
buy both of us!"

She loved to dream,
"I can see us over there in the showcase!
I can see us in hardcover!
I can see us in our tenth printing!"

". . . . .yeah. . . . ," I gazed.

I could feel the dream too.

Then one day a customer came by
and started looking through Calendar,

"This one's nice. It's just the right size."

Oh, she likes her!

Hey, look at me!

I'm small too!

I'm right here! Right next to h. . . . . .

"I'll take this calendar."

It was too late.
She chose her and didn't even notice me.

We barely had a chance to wave goodbye.

I was alone again.

A few days passed. . . .

which turned into weeks,

which felt like months.

I missed Calendar.

I turned to the self help section
hoping to make some new friends there...

THUNK!

**Somebody knocked me right off the counter
and left me lying on the floor!**

I was stepped on a bunch of times and
kicked a few more,
ouch!
Yow!
Oooh!
Ouch!

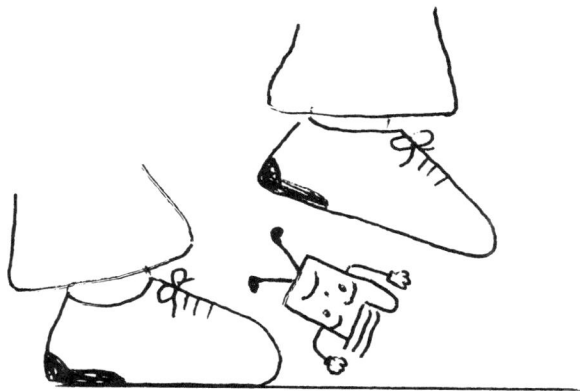

Things couldn't get much worse.

At that moment,

"My my. Now how did this get here?"

A store clerk found me!

She's going to put me back on display,
hooray!

Hey, where is she taking me?

The cookbook section?!

Hey, I'm not a cookbook!

Miss, wait!

I AM NOT A COOKBOOK!

She stuck me right between
The Giddy Gourmet and Mrs. Grill-it,

the two tallest books on the shelf!

Oh-no! Big books mean big teasing.

Here it comes, I warned myself.

"Well, hello there!
I'm Grill-it and this is Giddy.
And who are you?" she smiled.

"I. . . . I'm. . .My. . . ."
I was so shocked, I could barely speak.

Giddy quickly jumped in,
"Welcome to our shelf! Make yourself at
home."

They weren't like those other big books at
all.

They were friendly and warm,
just like Calendar!

I thought to myself. . . .

I'll never judge a book by its cover again.

We talked and talked.

I told them all about Calendar,
and how I fell off the shelf.

How I've been waiting
for weeks and weeks,
and still,

I haven't been bought.

"Weeks?!" Grill-it smiled and continued,
"We've been here for months!"

"Months?!" I couldn't believe it!
Longer than me!

"Yes," Giddy giggled,
"And oh, what fun we've had!"

"Waiting is fun?" I asked.

Grill-it explained,
"We've been sharing recipes
and making up new ones. . ."

Then Giddy jumped in and smiled,

"Waiting is cured through creating!"

"Now let's create a recipe with you, Pocket!"

"Sounds great to me!" I beamed.

Whoosh!
Suddenly I felt so thankful.

I felt thankful for
getting knocked off the shelf,
which lead me to the clerk,
who put me here in the wrong section,

which is exactly where I need to be!

"What's this little book?"

And wouldn't you know it?
As soon as I started counting
my blessings,

somebody pulled me right off the shelf.

I was nervous she would put me back,
once she realized I'm not a cookbook.

But instead, she skimmed me and giggled.

It felt wonderful to be noticed.

Buy me, oh please buy me, I hoped.

No sale.

Then another customer came by and skimmed me!

Again, the smile, the giggle!

This time they held and skimmed me all the way up to the front counter!

This is it!

No sale.

". . . . no one will ever buy you . . . ."

Those harsh words from the big books
haunted me.

Wait! Someone's picking me up!

Skimming . . .skimming.

Laughing! Laughing really hard!

Back down. No sale.

"Everyone who opens you smiles,"
a nearby voice said.

"Me?" I turned to find the mystery voice.

It was a pamphlet sitting to my right.

"Yes you.
I've noticed that you have a special way
with everyone who peeks at you."

"Oh, thank you Pamphlet.
But will I ever be bought?"

"Look Pocket," Pamphlet said,
"See that magazine over there?"

"Yes, I see him.
Why does he look so grumpy?"

"He's stuck on the buying thing,"
Pamphlet explained,

"That's all he thinks about.
But you are much wiser, my friend."

"I am?" I wondered.

"Yes! You make every moment count!

I've seen the way you create delight for
all the customers who skim you.

You don't push them or act know-it-all.
You just happily share yourself,

and they always leave with a smile."

"Oh thank you, Pamphlet!"
I squealed.

"Look kid," he assured me,
"I won't ever be bought.
I'm a pamphlet, I'm free!

What counts in life is what you make of it.
And you are making quite an impact!"

"...aaahhhh...," is all I could say.

Pamphlet was right.
It's time to start creating.

Just like Calendar and I used to do,
I made up a daydream.

I imagined that somebody wonderful was
about to read me,
from beginning to end.

I imagined and imagined.

I played the scene in my mind,
over and over.

Then I thought about my journey,

how much I had learned,

and how everything had happened
for a reason.

I felt so hopeful.

I just know somebody special
will read me soon.

I just know it.

And here you are!

<u>You</u> are that somebody special,
and I am so happy to live in your pocket!

You can read me anytime
or share me with a friend.

I'd like to help you create
your best self,

the way you just did with me.

When you gave me your attention,
you made me feel. . . . "wow!"

When you smiled,
I knew you believed in me.

You came along and gave me
just what I needed . . .

hope,
friendship and
the perfect pep talk.

Order THE POCKET PEP TALK From:

Goal Getters
3943 Chowen Ave. S.
Minneapolis, MN 55410

phone: **612-925-5814**
fax: **612-922-8241**
website: **www.Flirtnow.com**

Make checks payable to: Goal Getters,
$6.99 per book plus $1.00 shipping and
handling.